The International Family Law Practice 2016–2017

Fifth Edition

The International Family Law Practice 2016–2017

Fifth Edition

David Hodson OBE

Partner at The International Family Law Group LLP, London

English accredited family law solicitor, mediator, arbitrator, Deputy District Judge at the Central Family Court, London, Australian solicitor and barrister

With specialist contributions by:

Edward Bennett

Helen Blackburn

Nadine Finch

Louisa Ghevaert

Katharine Landells

Louise McCallum

Nazia Rashid

David Salter

Zimran Samuel

Timothy Scott QC

Ann Thomas

Aidan Vine QC

LexisNexis®

Published by LexisNexis

LexisNexis
Regus
Terrace Floor
Castlemead
Lower Castle Street
Bristol BS1 3AG

British Library Cataloguing-in-Publication Data

A catalogue record for this book is available from the British Library.

ISBN 978 1 78473 233 2

Typeset by Letterpart Limited, Caterham on the Hill, Surrey CR3 5XL

Printed and bound by CPI Group (UK) Ltd, Croydon, CR0 4YY

FOREWORD

The International Family Law Practice is a huge and impressive work and it is my continuing pleasure to write the Foreword to this edition. That this is already the 5th edition of a work first published in 2008 (then David Hodson's *A Practical Guide to International Family Law Practice*) bears testimony both to the continuing exponential growth in international family law litigation and to the success of and need for this work.

Since the publication of the 4th edition in 2015 there has been a plethora of CJEU and UK Supreme Court decisions and there is now beginning to be significant case law on the 1996 Hague Convention on the Protection of Children and the 2007 EU Maintenance Regulation. These developments are, of course, reflected in the new edition. But, as David Hodson says in his Preface, all these developments are to an extent overshadowed by the 23 June 2016 Referendum vote for the UK to leave the EU. As we write, the exact date of the exit is far from clear (though it is unlikely to be before March 2019) and the terms of the exit are unknown. It may be that the UK will seek to continue to be bound by some of the EU instruments governing Family Law, the revised Brussels II Regulation in particular, and it is to be noted that the UK has 'opted into' the negotiations to reform that instrument. But whatever the final outcome, the EU Regulations referred to in this work will continue to apply for some time yet.

In the past the Preface made the point that as so many practitioners now deal with international family law work it can no longer be considered a distinct specialisation. But that, however, is not to deny its complexity and it is the enduring strength of this work that it provides practitioners with a basic point of reference across the whole international family law field. *The International Family Law Practice* is squarely aimed at the practitioner and is replete with good practice advice and clarifying flowcharts. It is clearly written by a team of experienced practitioners, not least by David Hodson himself, whose long involvement in international practice was recognised by the award of an OBE in 2014.

An impressive feature of the work is its width of coverage. Its 30 chapters deal with not just the obvious issues such as recognition of foreign marriages and divorce, same-sex and cohabitation relationships, financial provision after an overseas divorce, marital agreements, child abduction, child relocation, surrogacy, international adoption but also less obvious but really useful topics

such as enforcement and registration of orders, stays in the UK, Europe and worldwide, pensions, trusts and forced marriage. There are also a number of useful practical chapters dealing with service, affidavits and statements of truth, evidence, cross-border alternative dispute resolution, international judicial collaboration and legal aid. The book also includes chapters on Islamic Law and immigration issues and a new chapter (Chapter 30) on FGM. The work begins with a couple of chapters explaining what international family law is and why practitioners need to know about it and also on practice and case management. The interesting concluding chapter looks to the future.

Not to be overlooked are the indispensable Appendices which not only contain the disparate relevant domestic and international legislation but also various Protocols and international Declarations. In short, *The International Family Law Practice* has established itself as an indispensable part of the practising family lawyer's library and an equally useful work of reference for the judiciary and the academic community.

Nigel Lowe
Emeritus Professor of Law, Cardiff University and Consultant to Number Fourteen of Gray's Inn Square
November 2016

PREFACE

Fairly early on the morning of Friday 24 June 2016, Family Law woke, went downstairs and turned on the television news, saw the percentages of the EU referendum vote on the screen, saw it was much closer than had been anticipated and was heading to make an early morning cup of coffee when a few words from the television didn't seem to make sense. Family Law paused and returned. Indeed it was closer than had been anticipated. But the closeness was not the point. The vote was to leave the EU. At which point everything changed; for Family Law both national and international, for our national law in general, for the UK and across the world.[1]

This fifth edition is being written only two months after the referendum yet so much has already happened in UK political life. Progress with legislative change has had to wait upon government and ministerial changes and then for civil servants to be briefed.[2] But some indications can already be given. Moreover this 5th edition will be regularly digitally updated until the intended 6th edition, probably in Autumn 2018, which will incorporate new legislation at the point of leaving the EU. In the meantime the UK has at least another two years of EU law continuing to apply, including new EU family laws, hence the importance of this edition.

In the fourth edition, it was said that the issues which family law faced with the EU were a microcosm of the UK relationship generally; an acknowledgement of the historic, commercial and cultural closeness with Europe, yet real anxieties about the direction, new laws and ambitions of the EU. The majority in the referendum voted to leave and the new Prime Minister, Theresa May MP, has made it clear this is what will happen. Family law will be part of this exit process. It will be a period of much change for the country, including for family law.

But certain elements will continue. Whatever happens about EU movement of people with the UK after departure, England and Wales will remain one of the most international countries in the world with very many international families from throughout the world living here and very many families from England and Wales living abroad. There will remain a huge need for international

1 Variously described as the biggest event for the UK since the Second World War and the biggest event for Europe since the fall of the Berlin Wall.

2 There seems very little indication of any planning, in the family law context and wider, before the referendum vote for specific steps that would be taken if the decision was to leave.

family law, and experienced practitioners. It may be that laws emanate from The Hague rather than Brussels but many will seem fairly similar[3] albeit having a global reach rather than separating the legal globe into the EU v non-EU.

Throughout its time as a member of the EU, the UK has had an ambivalent attitude. It has been looking across the Channel and the North Sea at continental Europe, yet has looked across the Atlantic and around the world at the very many countries with which the UK has always had and/or now has a very close connection. The UK is truly a global international country and not just a European country. In the family law context, the UK has very many family law connections around the world and probably more than any other EU member state. Moreover as the original common law jurisdiction, it has far closer connections with common law countries around the world than with the EU. The UK is a major innovator, creator and developer of family law trends, practices and ideas and is much followed around the world. The EU departure means this country will be free again[4] to enter into bilateral and multilateral treaties with non-EU countries, a cause of real opportunity for closer dealings with countries around the world.

The departure from the EU will be the opportunity for the UK to work with countries around the world to develop the best possible family law and practice for better outcomes for international families and their children.

The period since the previous edition has again seen many changes. Following the introduction of the unified Family Court there are also now specific rules for allocation of cases to High Court judges with certificates of complexity. We now have further case-law in respect of the EU Maintenance Regulation. There have been an increasing number of CJEU decisions of considerable importance including, crucially, the practical aspect of what lawyers have to do to gain priority of proceedings, lis pendens. We have added an extra chapter on FGM given its significance in the international family law context and I am grateful to the author, Zimran Samuel. I remain grateful to my previous contributors who have yet again agreed to write chapters.

The authors are Edward Bennett (international judicial collaboration), Helen Blackburn (adoption, legal aid and child abduction), Nadine Finch (immigration), Louisa Ghevaert (surrogacy), Katherine Landells (same-sex relationships), Louise McCallum (forced marriages), Nazia Rashid (Islamic issues), David Salter (marital agreements, trusts and pensions), Zimran Samuel (FGM), Tim Scott QC (general international children law matters), Ann Thomas (relocation) and Aidan Vine QC (public law). I have written the chapters on case/practice management, the European imperative in international family law, recognition of foreign marriages and divorces, stays of proceedings, domicile, residence and nationality, financial provision after an overseas divorce, international injunctions, enforcement and recognition of

3 Primarily because they were either drafted as part of the same law reform process or one was modelled on the other.

4 See 2.2.

financial orders, domestic violence, service, affidavits and statements of truth, evidence and ADR as well as the first three appendices.

My publishers, Greg Woodgate and Kate Hather, have been highly encouraging with good ideas for developing the book.

As ever, I am exceptionally grateful to my colleagues at The International Family Law Group LLP, London. Stuart Clark, Michael Allum and Emma Nash with Emma Chowdhury (web links) helped with a considerable amount of initial research. I appreciate the exceptionally fortunate position to be in a firm which day by day receives enquiries from around the world, including many law firms here and abroad, about the most incredibly complex of issues of law and practice. The interwoven facts, international connections and matters of law sometimes defy reasonable belief but this is the life of many international families. As I set out in the concluding chapter, I remain saddened that despite good intentions in many places the position for these families and their children is not getting easier.

I am exceedingly grateful to Professor Nigel Lowe for writing the Foreword.

I am particularly grateful to my wife, Ann, for all her considerable support without which this book would never have come into creation or been seen in its subsequent incarnations.

Finally and as an undoubted highlight for me, I was absolutely delighted in the Queen's Birthday Honours List in June 2014 to receive the OBE for '*services to international family law*'. I felt very strongly that it was because of the incredible work by many people in this area of which I have been most fortunate to be a part. Conversations with Her Majesty are supposed to be confidential but, at the risk of being carted off to the Tower, at the Investiture in early December 2014 at Windsor Castle one of the things Her Majesty said to me was, in terms, international family law sounds very complicated. Yes indeed, ma'am, it certainly is!

Thank you to Jordan Publishing for realising the importance of this work and the need for this book. It is a most interesting time to be involved in the international aspects of family law.

David Hodson OBE MICArb
September 2016

CONTENTS

Foreword		v
Preface		vii
Table of Cases		xxxiii
Table of Statutes		lxiii
Table of Statutory Instruments		lxxi
Table of International Legislation		lxxix
Abbreviations		xciii
PART 1		
Narrative		
Chapter 1		
Introduction and Case/Practice Management		3
Overview		3
1.1	Why do I need to know about international family law?	4
1.2	What is an international case?	5
1.3	When there is an international element in a case, what do I need to do?	6
1.4	But aren't financial outcomes across Europe (and other parts of the world) almost the same?	7
1.5	Worldwide differences in family law practice	9
1.6	Introduction to case/practice management	11
	Should the practice take on this 'international' case?	11
	Be prepared	14
1.7	What to consider at the first interview	15
1.8	Which court?	18
1.9	Working with foreign family lawyers	27
1.10	Wider issues for consideration in international cases	31
1.11	This book	32
Chapter 2		
The European Imperative in International Family Law		35
Overview		35
2.1	European Union involvement in family law	35
2.2	EU exclusive competency and universal application in family law issues	39
2.3	Which law? The challenge of applicable law	41

2.4 Which European court? 48
European Court of Justice 48
European Court of Human Rights 54
2.5 Impact of Brexit on family law 57
The new Brussels II 61

Chapter 3
Recognition of Foreign Marriages and Divorces 67
Overview 67
3.1 Introduction 67
3.2 Recognition of foreign marriages 68
Formalities 71
Permitted circumstances 71
The law of the place of celebration: '*lex loci celebrationis*' 72
Case-law including 'non-marriages' 74
Capacity 83
Ante nuptial domicile 83
Consent 86
Capacity exceptions 89
Other capacity issues 89
Royal marriages 90
Court procedure when there is a foreign marriage 90
Marriages in paradise 93
3.3 Polygamy (actual or potential) 94
Validity and capacity 94
Contents of the divorce petition 96
Some effects of polygamous marriage 97
3.4 Recognition of foreign divorces 98
Divorces, annulments and judicial separations granted in the UK 102
Divorces obtained outside the UK 102
Recognition of a divorce and similar family court orders within the EU 102
Non-recognition of EU divorces and similar family court orders 104
Procedure on recognition, registration and enforcement of EU divorces and other family court orders 106
Recognition of divorce outside BII countries by means of 'proceedings' 109
Proceedings 111
Recognition of divorces outside of UK obtained other than by means of proceedings 114
Transnational divorces 116
Non-recognition of divorces elsewhere 117
Refusal of recognition of foreign divorces by proceedings or non-proceedings 117
3.5 Declarations as to status 124

13.7 Conclusion 562

Chapter 14
Child Relocation 563
Overview 563
14.1 Introduction 563
14.2 Statute law and procedure 565
14.3 Developments in case-law 568
14.4 Pre-*Payne* (1970–2001) 569
14.5 *Payne* to *CK v MK* (2001–2011) 569
Payne 569
Post-*Payne* case-law 571
14.6 The turning tide: *MK v CK* (2011)–*Re F* (2015) 582
MK v CK 582
Post-*MK v CK* case-law 584
Re F 595
Post *Re F* case-law 596
14.7 The 1996 Hague Convention 600
14.8 Temporary removal from the jurisdiction 603
Entitlement to remove for up to one month 604
Temporary removal in the absence of statutory entitlement under s 13(1)(b) of the CA 605
Good practice 608
Case-law on temporary removals including holidays 609
14.9 Internal relocation within England and Wales and within the UK 620
Case-law 623
14.10 Costs in relocation cases 636
14.11 Preparation for relocation applications 637
14.12 The use of experts 639
14.13 Opposing a relocation application 640
14.14 Securing contact if a relocation is permitted 642
14.15 Anxiety about an abduction taking place 643
14.16 Steps to be taken if there is a fear of a non-return after any agreed foreign holiday or temporary relocation 644
14.17 Conclusion 647

Chapter 15
Child Abduction 653
Overview 653
15.1 Introduction 653
15.2 Criminal law 656
15.3 1980 Hague Convention 658
Background 658
Contents of the Convention 661
Rights of custody 664
Wrongful removal or retention 668
Habitual residence 668

	Hague Convention defences	670
	Consent or subsequent acquiescence: Article 13(a)	670
	Parent not actually exercising custody rights: Article 13(a)	672
	Grave risk of physical or psychological harm or place in an intolerable situation: Article 13(b)	673
	Objection of the child: Article 13	677
	Now settled in his/her new environment: Article 12	681
	ECtHR jurisprudence	682
	Other Hague Convention aspects	684
	Interim powers	685
	Procedure	685
15.4	Child abduction within the EU: BII revised	686
	Introduction	686
	Changes to the 1980 Hague Convention made by BII	687
	Trumping orders	689
	Recognition and enforcement of return orders	692
15.5	Hague Convention: outside of the EU	694
15.6	Non-Hague Convention country cases: abduction to this country	695
15.7	Non-Hague Convention country cases: abduction from this country	698
15.8	Bilateral agreements	701
	Anglo-Pakistan Protocol	701
	The Cairo Declaration	702
15.9	Procedure	702
	Introduction	702
	Procedure under the Hague Convention	703
	Non-Hague cases	707
	General provisions	708
	The out of hours judge	710
15.10	Practical action: the lawyer's role	712
	Professional obligations	712
	What to consider with the client from whom a child has been abducted	715
	What to consider with the client who fears the child may be abducted	718
	Using the media	719
15.11	'Reunite'	720
15.12	Acting for the party who has abducted the child to England	720
	Before proceedings begin	720
	When proceedings commence	721
15.13	Practical action: The court's powers	721
	Methods of locating a missing child	722
	Useful orders and declarations to obtain if a child is located abroad	723
	What orders and directions to seek and serve when the child has been located	723

Collection and location orders 724
All ports warnings 726
Court order prohibiting the child's removal from the jurisdiction 727
Wardship 727
Contempt 727
Sequestration proceedings 728

Chapter 16
International Adoption 731
Overview 731
16.1 Introduction 731
16.2 Forms of international adoptions 733
Convention adoption 733
An overseas adoption 733
A foreign adoption recognised by the law of England and Wales and effected under the law of another country 734
A foreign adoption not recognised by the law of England and Wales 736
Adoption overseas 736
16.3 Procedure and good practice 736
16.4 History of intercountry adoption in this country 737
16.5 The Convention 738
Requirements 740
Recognition and effect 742
Full and simple adoptions 742
General provisions 743
Local authority obligations and practice 743
16.6 Practice and process of approval and matching for intercountry adoption 743
16.7 Applications for adoptions orders concerning foreign children in the UK 746
Application for a Convention adoption order 746
Application for English adoption order 746
16.8 Miscellaneous issues when non-compliance 748
16.9 Immigration law and nationality 749
A child subject to a Convention adoption effected in the State of origin 750
A child adopted by Convention adoption order made in the UK as the receiving State or full Convention adoption order is made in the State of origin after the child has entered the UK 750
A child adopted by overseas adoption order made in a designated list country 750
A foreign child adopted in the UK 751
16.10 Assistance 752

Chapter 17
Surrogacy 753
Overview 753
17.1 Introduction 754
17.2 The Surrogacy Arrangements Act 1985 756
17.3 The Human Fertilisation and Embryology Act 1990 757
17.4 The Human Fertilisation and Embryology Act 2008 757
Parenthood 757
Parental order requirements and process 758
17.5 Case-law 760
Allocation and guidance on parental order reports 760
Death 761
Domicile 761
Consent 766
Payments and public policy 770
Six month deadline 775
Legal difficulties 781
Married surrogate 782
17.6 Enduring family relationship 784
17.7 Child's name 785
17.8 Child arrangements orders and surrogacy 785
17.9 Adoption in a surrogacy context 786
17.10 Surrogacy applicants from abroad 788
17.11 The Hague on surrogacy 788
17.12 Maternity and paternity rights 790

Chapter 18
Forced Marriage 791
Overview 791
18.1 Introduction 791
18.2 Applications by third parties 794
18.3 Orders 795
18.4 The Forced Marriage Unit 796
18.5 Practical considerations 796
18.6 Pre-existing remedies 798
18.7 Case-law 800
18.8 Procedure 803
18.9 Further developments 803

Chapter 19
Care and Placement Proceedings involving International Families 805
Overview 805
19.1 The international framework 806
19.2 Jurisdiction 809
Brussels II Revised 812
The 1996 Hague Convention 819
Brussels II Revised versus 1996 Hague Convention 823
Jurisdiction at common law 823

19.3 Transfers of jurisdiction and stays 825
Art 15 transfers to other EU member states (save Denmark) under Brussels II Revised – general principles 826
Art 15 transfers to other EU member states (save Denmark) under Brussels II Revised – factual application so far 832
Art 15 transfers to other EU member states (save Denmark) under Brussels II Revised – procedure 834
Art 8 transfers to other 1996 Hague Convention contracting parties 837
Stays at common law on the grounds of *forum conveniens* 838
19.4 Co-operation, the Central Authorities and cross-border placements under Brussels II revised and the 1996 Hague Convention 840
Co-operation and the Central Authorities under Brussels II Revised 840
Cross-border placements under Brussels II Revised 842
Co-operation, the Central Authorities and cross-border placement under the 1996 Hague Convention 843
The proper limits of the functions of the Central Authorities 845
19.5 Applicable law and the 1996 Hague Convention 846
General structure as to applicable law 847
Parental responsibility and applicable law 847
Provisos, riders and clarifications 848
Application to care and placement proceedings 849
19.6 Giving notice to parental responsibility holders under the laws of other states and to respondents who are overseas 850
19.7 The obligation to notify consular authorities 852
19.8 Case management and directions for overseas evidence and assessments 853
Allocation/level of court 854
Evidence overseas 855
Assessments 856
19.9 Placement overseas, immigration and recognition/enforcement of orders 858
Structuring the right order 859
Immigration 860
Recognition/enforcement of orders 861
Striking the right balance 862

Chapter 20
Domestic Violence 863
Overview 863
20.1 Domestic violence: a European problem? 863
20.2 Policy and legislative response 865
20.3 The Istanbul Convention 867
20.4 The EU Victim's Directive 868
20.5 The 2011 Criminal and 2013 Civil European Protection Orders 869

20.6	Directive 2011/99/EU of the European Parliament and of the Council of 13 December 2011 on the European Protection Order (in criminal matters)	869
20.7	Regulation 606/2013 of the European Parliament and of the Council of 12 June 2013 on Mutual Recognition of Protection measures in Civil Matters	874
20.8	Domestic rules	879
20.9	The future	883

Chapter 21
Service 885

Overview		885
21.1	Introduction	885
21.2	Service under Brussels II and other EU legislation	892
21.3	Service in accordance with the EU Service Regulation	896
21.4	Service in accordance with The Hague Service Convention	901
21.5	Service through foreign governments, judicial authorities and British consular authorities	903
21.6	Time for service abroad	903
21.7	Service in England of foreign court orders	905

Chapter 22
Affidavits, Statements of Truth and Apostilles 907

Overview		907
22.1	Introduction	907
22.2	Affidavit or statement of truth?	908
22.3	Requirements in respect of affidavits in the international context	910
22.4	Legalisation of documents, an Apostille	911

Chapter 23
Evidence 915

Overview		915
23.1	Orders for disclosure	915
23.2	Evidence by deposition	916
23.3	Evidence from abroad	917
	Letters of request: General	917
	The Hague Taking of Evidence Convention	920
	Letters of request within Europe	923
	Norwich Pharmacal orders	924
23.4	Video link, Skype and other electronic evidence	925
23.5	Evidence of foreign law	932
23.6	Evidence in England to assist foreign courts	933
23.7	Evidence from the Home Office	934
23.8	Evidence and dealings with non-English speaking witnesses	934
23.9	Evidence and assistance via British Embassies and High Commissions abroad	937

Iran 1012
Saudi Arabia 1013
Egypt 1014
Pakistan 1015

Chapter 27
Immigration Issues 1017
Overview 1017
27.1 Introduction 1017
27.2 History of immigration controls 1018
Controlling entry to the UK 1019
27.3 Categories in which individuals can remain in the UK 1021
Illegal entry 1022
The right to British citizenship for a child born here 1023
Children born in the UK 1024
Unaccompanied and separated children 1025
Rights under the EU Treaty 1026
The Convention relating to the status of refugees 1027
European Convention on Human Rights 1027
The United Nations Convention on the Rights of the Child 1027
27.4 The interface between immigration and family law 1028
Importance of one or more family member being British 1031
Support for parties during family proceedings 1031
Obtaining immigration status for duration of family proceedings 1033
Entitlement to legal aid 1033

Chapter 28
International Judicial Collaboration 1035
Overview 1035
28.1 Introduction 1035
28.2 Circumstances for using judicial collaboration 1037
28.3 Initiating judicial collaboration 1043
Judicial networks: formal and informal 1043
Requesting judicial collaboration: the process 1045
Bias and recusal 1048
Established use of judicial collaboration in England and Wales 1049
Judicial collaboration and the USA 1053
Judicial collaboration and the Netherlands 1054

Chapter 29
Female Genital Mutilation 1057
Overview 1057
29.1 Introduction 1057
International framework 1057
Definition 1058
Current legislative provisions 1059

29.2	Extension of extra-territorial jurisdiction	1060
29.3	Female genital mutilation protection order	1060
	The girl or women to be protected	1061
	Relevant third party	1061
	Any other person	1061
	Grounds for making an order	1062
	Duration of the order	1062
	Terms of the order	1062
	Respondents	1062
	Ex parte hearings	1063
	Breach	1063
	Statistical progress	1064
29.4	Case-law and practical considerations	1064
	Mandatory reporting	1067

Chapter 30
The Future 1069

30.1	Introduction	1069
30.2	Future developments: the UK leaving the EU	1070
30.3	Future developments: the common law versus the civil law	1072
30.4	Future developments: international family lawyers need ...	1075
30.5	Future developments: international families need ...	1075
30.6	Conclusion	1076

PART 2
Supporting Materials

Appendix 1
England Expects ... Not to be Confused with Scotland! – A Guide to Family Law in the British Isles **1081**

Appendix 2
A Forum Checklist **1087**

Appendix 3
Websites **1091**

PART 3
Domestic Legislation and Materials

Appendix 4
Adoption (Intercountry Aspects) Act 1999, including the Hague 1993 Adoption Convention **1097**

Appendix 5
Adoption and Children Act 2002 **1109**

Appendix 6
Care Planning, Placement and Case Review (England) Regulations 2010 SI 2010/959, regs 3–6 and 12 1127

Appendix 7
Child Abduction and Custody Act 1985 1131

Appendix 8
Children Act 1989, Sch 2, para 19 1149

Appendix 9
Children and Families Act 2014, Pt 7 1151

Appendix 10
Civil Partnership Act 2004, ss 212–238, Sch 20 1181

Appendix 11
Domicile and Matrimonial Proceedings Act 1973 1197

Appendix 12
Family Law Act 1986 1207

Appendix 13
Family Law Act 1996, Pt 4A 1235

Appendix 14
Family Procedure Rules 2010 and Supplementary Practice Directions, SI 2010/2955 1245

Appendix 15
Human Fertilisation and Embryology Act 2008, ss 33, 35, 54 1407

Appendix 16
Marriage (Same Sex Couples) Act 2013, ss 1, 9–11 1411

Appendix 17
Matrimonial and Family Proceedings Act 1984, Pt III 1415

Appendix 18
President's Guidance – Communicating with the Home Office in Family Proceedings (April 2013) 1427

Appendix 19
Surrogacy Arrangements Act 1985 1429

PART 4
EU Regulations and Directives and Related European Legislation

Appendix 20
EU Brussels I Recast 1215/2012 1437

Appendix 21
EU Brussels II Revised 2201/2003 1467

Appendix 22
Practice Guide for the Application of the Brussels IIa Regulation 1503

Appendix 23
EU Applicable Law Regulation 1259/2010 1569

Appendix 24
EU Enforcement Order for Uncontested Claims 805/2004 1579

Appendix 25
EU Legal Aid Directive 2002/8 1593

Appendix 26
EC Lisbon Treaty 2007, Art 81 1605

Appendix 27
EU Maintenance Regulation 4/2009 1607

Appendix 28
EU Mediation Directive 2008/52 1641

Appendix 29
EU Regulation No 606/2013 on Mutual Recognition of Protection Measures in Civil Matters 1649

Appendix 30
EU Directive of 2011/99 on the European Protection Order 1661

Appendix 31
EU Service Regulation 1393/2007 1677

Appendix 32
EU Taking of Evidence Regulation 1206/2001 1689

Appendix 33
EU Directive 2012/29 on the Rights, Support and Protection of Victims of Crime 1701

Appendix 34
Lugano Convention 2007/712/EC 1725

Appendix 35
Strasbourg Legal Aid Agreement 1977 1765

Appendix 36
Council of Europe Convention on Preventing and Combating Violence Against Women and Domestic Violence – the Istanbul Convention 1769

Appendix 37
European 1980 Convention on Recognition and Enforcement of Decisions concerning Custody of Children and on Restoration of Custody of Children – the Luxembourg 1980 Convention 1795

Appendix 38
Vienna Convention on Consular Relations 1963, arts 36 and 37 1805

PART 5
The Hague Conventions and Related Materials

Appendix 39
The Hague 1980 Child Abduction Convention 1809

Appendix 40
Hague 2007 Convention on the International Recovery of Child Support and Other Forms of Family Maintenance 1813

Appendix 41
Guide to Good Practice under the Hague Convention of 25 October 1980 on the Civil Aspects of International Child Abduction: Mediation 1839

Appendix 42
Hague 1996 Convention on Jurisdiction, Applicable Law, Recognition, Enforcement and Co-operation in respect of Parental Responsibility and Means for Protection of the Child 1941

Appendix 43
Explanatory Report on the 1996 Hague Convention 1957

Appendix 44
Department of Education Advice for Local Authorities and Others on Cross-border Child Protection Cases under the 1996 Hague Convention 1993

Appendix 45
Hague 1965 Convention on the Service Abroad of Judicial and Extrajudicial Documents in Civil or Commercial Matters 2013

Appendix 46
Hague 1970 Convention on the Taking of Evidence Abroad in Civil or Commercial Matters 2021

Appendix 47
Emerging Guidance regarding the Development of the International Hague Network of Judges and General Principles for Judicial Communications including Commonly Accepted Safeguards for Direct Judicial Communications in Specific Cases, within the Context of the International Hague Network of Judges 2031

PART 6
Other Materials

Appendix 48
Cairo Declaration of 17 January 2005 2045

Appendix 49
UK Pakistan Protocol Child Abduction Protocol 2047

Appendix 50
Muslim Family Law Ordinance 1961 2049

Appendix 51
United Nations Convention on the Rights of the Child 1989 2055

Appendix 52
Washington Declaration on International Family Relocation 2010 2073

Index 2077